Spelling for Writing

• • • • • • • • • • • • • • • • • • Contents • • • • • • • • • • • • • • • • • • •

continued

Consonant Sounds and Letters

Bb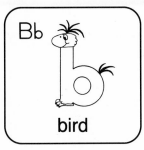
bird

Cc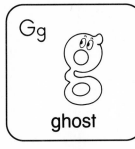
cat

Dd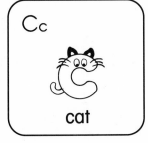
dinosaur

Ff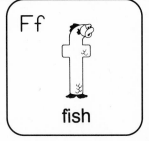
fish

Gg
ghost

Hh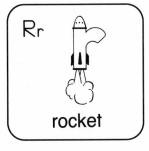
horse

Jj
jack-in-the-box

Kk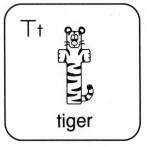
king

Ll
lion

Mm
monster

Nn
nurse

Pp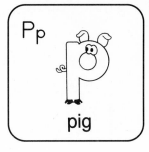
pig

Qq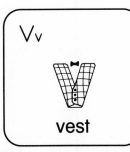
queen

Rr
rocket

Ss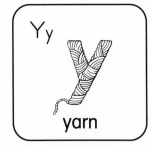
seal

Tt
tiger

Vv
vest

Ww
worm

Yy
yarn

Zz
zebra

Vowel Sounds and Letters

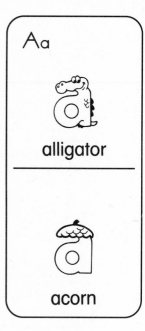

Aa

alligator

acorn

Ee

elephant

eel

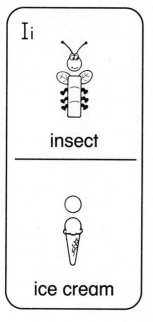

Ii

insect

ice cream

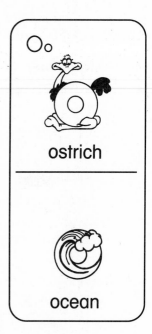

Oo

ostrich

ocean

Uu

umbrella

unicorn

Bookworm Spelling for Writing

MAKING YOUR SPELLING NOTEBOOK

1

You can make your own Spelling Notebook to use when you write.

2

Find the pages at the back of this book that have the 📓 in the corner. Pull them out.

3

Print your name and draw a picture on the cover. You may want to paste it to a sheet of colored paper. You can make a back cover too.

4

Ask your teacher to help you put your Spelling Notebook together.

How to Study a Word

1 **LOOK** at the word. Name and touch each letter.

2 **SAY** the word.

3 **THINK** about the word.

4 **WRITE** the word.

5 **CHECK** the spelling.

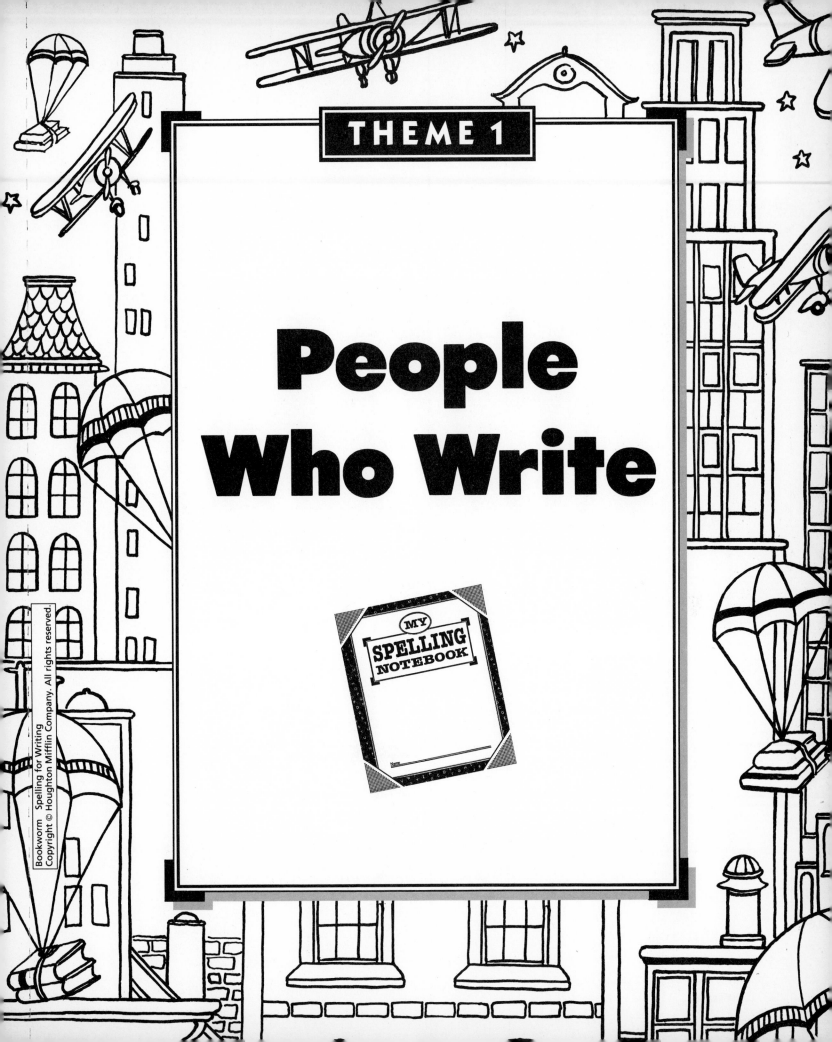

THEME 1

People Who Write

MY SPELLING NOTEBOOK

Name

Name _____

1 The Long a Sound Spelled ay

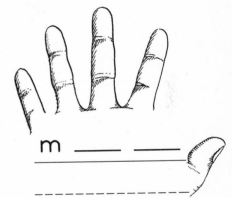
LOOK at and **SAY** the words.

THINK about the words. Each word has the long **a** sound. It is the first sound in ⓐ.

✏ **WRITE** the missing letters to spell the 🌰 sound. Then write each Spelling Word.

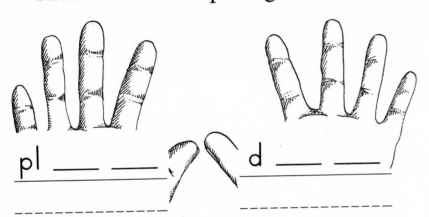

pl _ _ _

1. _____

d _ _ _

3. _____

m _ _ _

5. _____

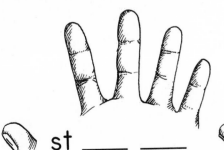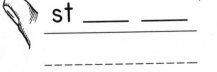

st _ _ _

2. _____

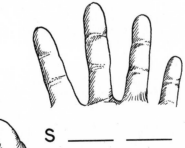

s _ _ _

4. _____

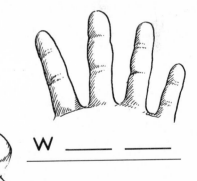

w _ _ _

6. _____

✏ **WRITE** the Spelling Word that begins like each picture name.

7. _____

8. 👤 _____

CHECK the spelling of each word you wrote.

Skill: Children study the spellings of words with the /ā/ sound spelled
ay. **Magic Picture: acorn**

Theme 1 People Who Write
JIMMY LEE DID IT   **9**

Name _____

Spelling and Meaning

SPELLING WORDS		
way	day	play
say	stay	may

Write each word under the correct letter in your Spelling Notebook.

 Write the Spelling Word for each clue.

1. not work

2. not leave

3. not night

1. _____ **2.** _____ **3.** _____

Proofreading

 Circle three Spelling Words that are wrong.
Write each word correctly.

WANTED: JIMMY LEE

People sai he makes a mess.

He mae even play tricks on you!

Do you know a wey to catch him?

4. _____ **5.** _____ **6.** _____

Skill: Children study the meanings of and proofread for spelling errors in words with the |ā| sound spelled *ay.*

Writer's Words from the Story

Writer's Words

who   come   know

Write each word under the correct letter in your Spelling Notebook.

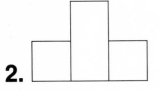 Write the correct Writer's Words.

1. 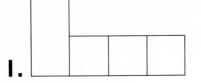 _____

2. _____

3.  _____

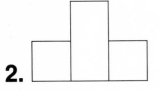 Write the missing Writer's Words.

4. I'll find out _____ he is.

5. I _____ just what to do.

6. He will _____ to get this soon!

Skill: Children study the spellings and meanings of high-frequency words.

Theme 1 People Who Write
JIMMY LEE DID IT   **11**

Spelling and Writing

SPELLING WORDS		
way	day	play
say	stay	may

Writer's Words

who come
know

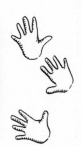

✏️ Pretend you are a detective. Write a question you might ask to help solve each mystery. Use some list words.

1.

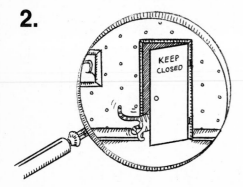

_____

_____

_____

_____

2.

KEEP
CLOSED

_____

_____

_____

3.

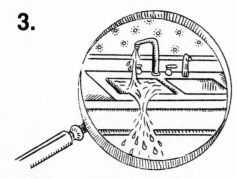

_____

_____

_____

📓 Write any hard words correctly in your Spelling Notebook.

Skill: Children write questions, using Spelling Words and Writer's Words from the Story.

SPELLING WORDS

eat	team
read	seat
each	clean

 Your Own Words

2 The Long e Sound Spelled ea

LOOK at and **SAY** the words.

THINK about the words. Each word has the long **e** sound. It is the first sound in.

▶ Find out what Snooper smells.
Color each part that has a word with the sound.

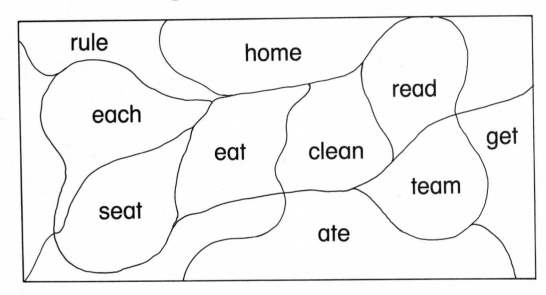

▶ **WRITE** the Spelling Words from the parts you colored.

1. _____   3. _____   5. _____

2. _____   4. _____   6. _____

▶ Draw a line under the letters that spell the sound
in each word you wrote.

CHECK the spelling of each word you wrote.

Skill: Children study the spellings of words with the |ē| sound spelled *ea.* **Magic Picture: eel**

Theme 1 People Who Write
MY FIVE SENSES   **13**

My Five Senses

Spelling and Meaning

SPELLING WORDS

| eat | read | each |
| team | seat | clean |

Write each word under the correct letter in your Spelling Notebook.

✏️ Write the missing Spelling Words.

1. You lie in a bed.
You sit in a ____.

_____

2. You watch a movie.
You ____ a book.

_____

3. You drink milk.
You ____ cheese.

_____

Proofreading

✏️ Circle three Spelling Words that are wrong.
Write each word correctly.

How to Play
- Please read every rule.
- Be sure your hands are clene.
- Feel what is on each plate.
- Guess right to help your tem.

smell
touch

4. _____

5. _____

6. _____

Skill: Children study the meanings of and proofread for spelling errors in words with the /ē/ sound spelled *ea*.

Writer's Words from the Story

Writer's Words

or   how   because

Write each word under the correct letter in your Spelling Notebook.

✎ Write the Writer's Word for each clue.

1. It begins like .

2. It rhymes with for.

3. It rhymes with  .

1. _____   2. _____   3. _____

✎ Write the missing Writer's Words.

4. Guess _____ many senses Bear uses.

5. Does he hear _____ see the bee?

6. He runs _____ he feels the bee!

Skill: Children study the spellings and meanings of high-frequency words.

Theme 1 People Who Write
MY FIVE SENSES   **15**

Name _____ Lesson **2**

Spelling and Writing

SPELLING WORDS

eat	read	each
team	seat	clean

Writer's Words

or	how
because	

✏️ How does Snooper use his senses? Write a sentence about each picture. Use some list words.

1.

_____

_____

_____

_____

2.

_____

_____

_____

_____

3.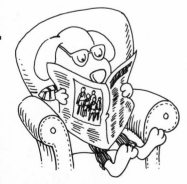

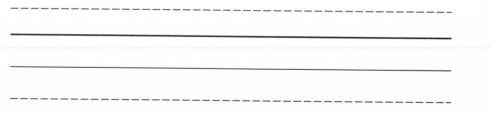

_____

_____

_____

_____

 Write any hard words correctly in your Spelling Notebook.

Skill: Children write captions for pictures, using Spelling Words and Writer's Words from the Story.

legs   cakes
bats   games
seats   kites

 Your Own Words

Name _____

3 Adding s to Naming Words

LOOK at and **SAY** the words.

THINK about the words. What letter makes these naming words mean more than one?

Look at the presents in the window. Color the pictures that go with each Spelling Word.

WRITE the Spelling Words that name the pictures you colored. Then draw a line under the letter that makes each word mean more than one.

1. _____

2. _____

3. _____

4. _____

5. _____

6. _____

CHECK the spelling of each word you wrote.

Skill: Children study the spellings of nouns whose plural is formed by adding -s.

Theme 1 People Who Write
THE SURPRISE   **17**

Spelling and Meaning

SPELLING WORDS		
legs	bats	seats
cakes	games	kites

Write each word under the correct letter in your Spelling Notebook.

✏️ Write the Spelling Word for each clue.

1. You can wear pants on them.
2. You can fly them.
3. You can hit balls with them.

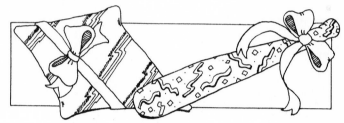

1. _____   2. _____   3. _____

Proofreading

✏️ Circle three Spelling Words that are wrong.
   Write each word correctly.

The kakes burned. Then two seates broke. The kites were lost, and the gams got mixed up. We had lots of fun anyway.

4. _____   5. _____   6. _____

Skill: Children study the meanings of and proofread for spelling errors in nouns whose plural is formed by adding -s.

Writer's Words from the Story

Writer's Words
old   only   right

Write each word under the correct letter in your Spelling Notebook.

✏️ Write the correct Writer's Words.

1. [puzzle grid] _____

2. [puzzle grid] _____

3. [puzzle grid] _____

✏️ Write the missing Writer's Words.

_____

4. I opened my present _____ away.

_____

5. I thought I had _____ one doll!

_____

6. I'm _____ enough to share my toy.

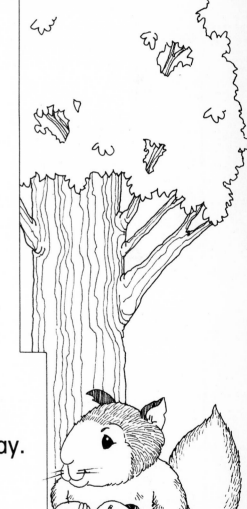

Skill: Children study the spellings and meanings of high-frequency words.

Theme 1 People Who Write
THE SURPRISE   **19**

Name _____ Lesson **3**

Spelling and Writing

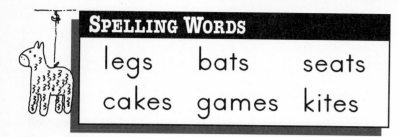

SPELLING WORDS		
legs	bats	seats
cakes	games	kites

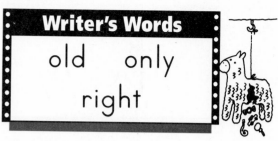

Writer's Words
old   only
right

Pretend that you made a piñata for your birthday party. Draw a picture of the piñata.

Write sentences that tell about the piñata and the surprises inside. Use some list words.

 Write any hard words correctly in your Spelling Notebook.

20 *Theme 1 People Who Write*
THE SURPRISE

Skill: Children write a description, using Spelling Words and Writer's Words from the Story.

Bookworm Spelling for Writing
Copyright © Houghton Mifflin Company. All rights reserved.

Name _____ Lesson **4**

Spelling Spree

SPELLING WORDS LESSON 1

way	day	play
say	stay	may

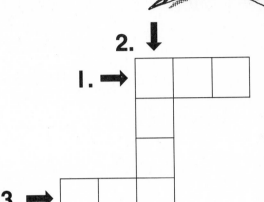

✏️ Write the Writer's Word for each clue.

1. What did you ____ to me?

2. Please ____ for lunch.

3. I know the ____ home.

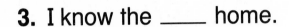

2. ↓
1. →
3. →

✏️ Write the Spelling Word that fits the clue and rhymes with the word in **dark print**.

4. It was cloudy all morning.
It was a **gray** ____.

5. I might give you money.
I ____ **pay**.

6. We have fun in the barn.
We ____ in **hay**.

Words That Rhyme
day
say

4. _____

5. _____

6. _____

Skill: Children review the spellings and meanings of words with the
|ā| sound spelled *ay*. *See also* the Word Builder on page 63.

Theme 1 People Who Write

Name _____ Lesson **4**

Spelling Spree

SPELLING WORDS LESSON 2

| eat | read | each |
| team | seat | clean |

✏️ Write the missing Spelling Words. Each important word in the sentence should begin with the same letter.

_____

_ _ _ _ _ _ _ _ _ _ _ _

I. Sam sat on Sid's _____ .

_____

_ _ _ _ _ _ _ _ _ _ _ _

2. Ellen and Eva _____ eggs.

_____

_ _ _ _ _ _ _ _ _ _ _ _

3. Tina's _____ took a turn.

_____

_ _ _ _ _ _ _ _ _ _ _ _

4. Ruth and Roy _____ riddles.

_____

_ _ _ _ _ _ _ _ _ _ _ _

5. Clowns _____ the clicking clocks.

_____

_ _ _ _ _ _ _ _ _ _ _ _

6. Ed enters at eight _____ evening.

Skill: Children review the spellings and meanings of words with the |ē| sound spelled *ea*. *See also* the Word Builders on pages 64–65.

Name _____ Lesson **4**

Spelling Spree

SPELLING WORDS LESSON 3
legs   bats   seats
cakes   games   kites

✎▷ Write the Spelling Word for each clue. Use the letters in the boxes to answer the riddle.

1. They have tails. __ __ ☐ __ __

2. You sit on them. __ __ ☐ __ __

3. You walk on them. ☐ __ __ __

4. You eat them. __ __ __ ☐ __

5. You play them. __ __ __ __ ☐

6. You swing them in a game. __ __ __ __

Riddle: What do you call giant stories?

tall __ __ __ __ __

Skill: Children review the spellings and meanings of nouns whose plural is formed by adding -s. *See also* the Word Builder on page 66.

Name _____ **Lesson 4**

Writer's Words Review

Writer's Words

who   come   know   or   how
because   old   only   right

✏️ Help Tanya mail her letter. Use ABC order.

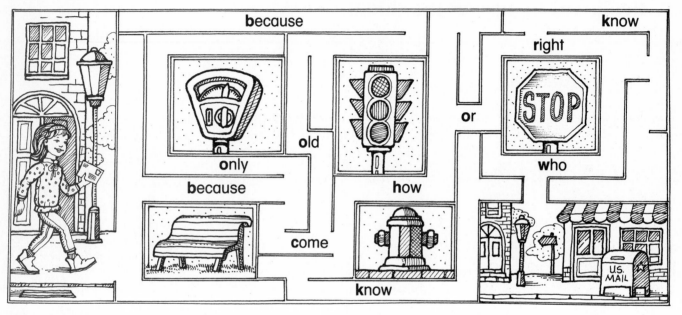

✏️ Write the Writer's Words from Tanya's path in ABC order.

1. _____   2. _____   3. _____

4. _____   5. _____   6. _____

✏️ Write the Writer's Words that have the sound.

7. _____   8. _____   9. _____

Skill: Children review the spellings of high-frequency words.

Old Favorites

MY
SPELLING
NOTEBOOK

Name

Name _____

5 The Vowel Sound in book

LOOK at and **SAY** the words.

THINK about the words. Each word has the vowel sound you hear in .

✏️ **WRITE** the missing letters to spell the sound.

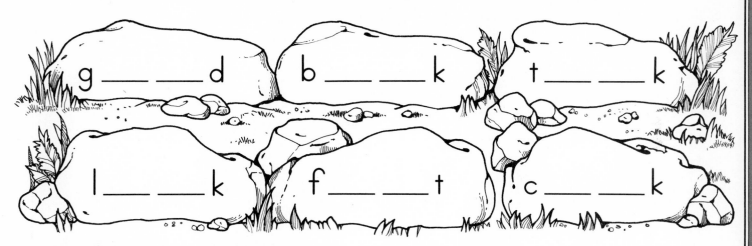

g _____ d   b _____ k   t _____ k

l _____ k   f _____ t   c _____ k

✏️ **WRITE** the Spelling Word from each stone.

1. _____   3. _____   5. _____

2. _____   4. _____   6. _____

✏️ **WRITE** the Spelling Word that ends like each picture name.

7.  _____   8. 🚤 _____

CHECK the spelling of each word you wrote.

Skill: Children study the spellings of words with the |o͝o| sound spelled *oo.*

Theme 2 Old Favorites
STONE SOUP

27

Stone Soup

Spelling and Meaning

SPELLING WORDS		
took	good	cook
foot	book	look

Write each word under the correct letter in your Spelling Notebook.

✏️ Write the missing Spelling Words.

_____

- - - - - - - - - - - - - - -

1. hand and _____

_____

- - - - - - - - - - - - - - -

2. _____ and bad

_____

- - - - - - - - - - - - - - -

3. gave and _____

Proofreading

✏️ Circle three Spelling Words that are wrong.
   Write each word correctly.

Super Soup

Learn to cuk good soup!

Read this booke!

Buy it, or lok for it

in your library!

4. _____
- - - - - - - - - - -
_____

5. _____
- - - - - - - - - - -
_____

6. _____
- - - - - - - - - - -

Skill: Children study the meanings of and proofread for spelling errors in words with the /oo/ sound spelled *oo*.

Writer's Words from the Story

Writer's Words

went house water

Write each word under the correct letter in your Spelling Notebook.

✏️ Write the correct Writer's Words.

1. 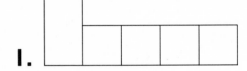   _____

2. 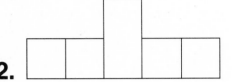    _____

3. 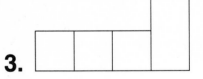   _____

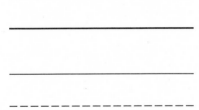

✏️ Write the missing Writer's Words.

_____

4. I had lunch at Nana's _____ .

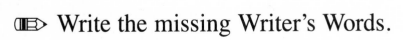

5. I _____ with my mom and dad.

6. We used carrots, peas, and _____ to make soup.

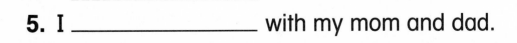

Skill: Children study the spellings and meanings of high-frequency words.

Theme 2 Old Favorites
STONE SOUP

Spelling and Writing

SPELLING WORDS

took good cook
foot book look

Writer's Words

went house
water

✎ Stone soup does not sound very tasty! Pretend you made some for your friends. Write sentences to tell why they should try it. Use some list words.

_____

- -

_____

- -

_____

- -

_____

- -

_____

- -

_____

 Write any hard words correctly in your Spelling Notebook.

Skill: Children write a persuasive paragraph, using Spelling Words and Writer's Words from the Story.

Name _____

6 The Vowel Sound in moon

LOOK at and **SAY** the words.

THINK about the words. Each word
has the vowel sound you hear in 🌙 .

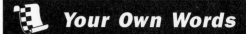 **Your Own Words**

✏️ Color each part that has a word with the 🌙 sound.

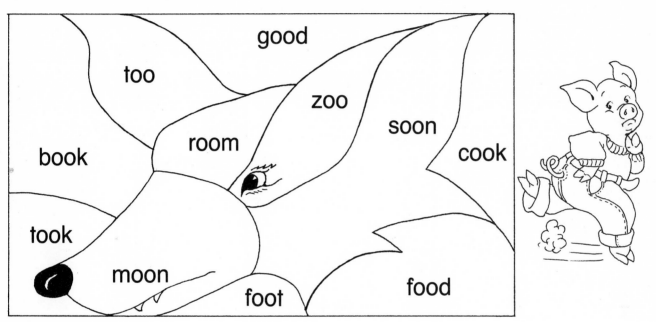

good

too

zoo

room

soon

book

cook

took

moon

foot

food

✏️ **WRITE** the Spelling Words from the parts you colored.

1. _____

2. _____

3. _____

4. _____

5. _____

6. _____

✏️ Draw a line under the letters that spell the 🌙 sound
in each word you wrote.

CHECK the spelling of each word you wrote.

Skill: Children study the spellings of words with the $|\overline{oo}|$ sound
spelled *oo*.

Theme 2 Old Favorites
THE THREE LITTLE PIGS   **31**

The Three Little Pigs

Spelling and Meaning

SPELLING WORDS		
soon	too	food
zoo	room	moon

Write each word under the correct letter in your Spelling Notebook.

✏️➤ Write the missing Spelling Words.

1. In the morning, I see the sun.
   At night, I see the ____.

   _____

   _____

2. You drink water.
   You eat ____.

   _____

   _____

3. You see cows at a farm.
   You see tigers at a ____.

   _____

Proofreading

✏️➤ Circle three Spelling Words that are wrong.
   Write each word correctly.

Dear Little Pig,

   Please come to my rume.
You will find good food there.
Come as soone as you can.
Bring your brothers tu!

                    The Wolf

4. ---------------

   _____

5. ---------------

   _____

6. _____

Skill: Children study the meanings of and proofread for spelling errors in words with the |oo| sound spelled *oo*.

Writer's Words from the Story

Writer's Words

first   thing   long

Write each word under the correct letter in your Spelling Notebook.

✏️ Write the Writer's Word for each clue.

_____

1. It rhymes with sing. _____

2. It begins like 🦁. _____

3. It begins like 🐟. _____

✏️ Write the missing Writer's Words.

_____

4. This is my _____ fair.

5. I have walked a _____ way.

6. What is that round _____ ?

Skill: Children study the spellings and meanings of high-frequency words.

Spelling and Writing

SPELLING WORDS		
soon	too	food
zoo	room	moon

Writer's Words
first thing long

✏️▷ Pretend you are the wolf in **The Three Little Pigs**. Write the story as the wolf would tell it. Use some list words.

I _____

_____

_____

_____

_____

_____

_____

_____

_____

🖍▷ Draw a picture to go with your story.

 Write any hard words correctly in your Spelling Notebook.

Skill: Children write a story, using Spelling Words and Writer's Words from the Story.

7 The Long i Sound Spelled y

LOOK at and **SAY** the words.

THINK about the words. Each word has the long **i** sound. It is the first sound in .

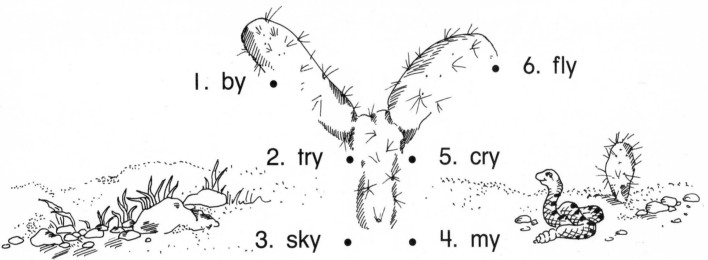

Draw a line from dot to dot
to find a letter that spells the sound.
Then draw a line under this letter in each word.

1. by
2. try
3. sky
4. my
5. cry
6. fly

WRITE the Spelling Word that begins like each picture name.

1.  _____

2.  _____

3.  _____

4.  _____

5.  _____

6.  _____

CHECK the spelling of each word you wrote.

Skill: Children study the spellings of words with the |ī| sound spelled y. **Magic Picture: ice cream**

Baby Rattlesnake

Spelling and Meaning

SPELLING WORDS		
my	by	cry
try	fly	sky

Write each word under the correct letter in your Spelling Notebook.

✏️ Write the Spelling Word for each clue.

next to   where stars shine   a sad sound

_____   _____   _____

_____   _____   _____

1. _____   2. _____   3. _____

Proofreading

✏️ Circle three Spelling Words that are wrong.
Write each word correctly.

4. _____

_____

5. _____

_____

6. _____

Theme 2 Old Favorites
BABY RATTLESNAKE

Skill: Children study the meanings of and proofread for spelling errors in words with the |ī| sound spelled *y*.

Writer's Words from the Story

Writer's Words

people want where

Write each word under the correct letter in your Spelling Notebook.

✏️ Write the correct Writer's Words.

1. _____

2. _____

3. _____

✏️ Write the missing Writer's Words.

_____

4. Here come some _____ .

_____

5. I _____ to scare them.

_____

6. I know _____ to hide!

Skill: Children study the spellings and meanings of high-frequency words.

Theme 2 Old Favorites
BABY RATTLESNAKE **37**

Spelling and Writing

SPELLING WORDS		
my	by	cry
try	fly	sky

Writer's Words

people want
where

Pretend Baby Rattlesnake wants to learn to fly. Write a poem that tells what he might say. Use some list words.

Draw a picture to go with your poem.

 Write any hard words correctly in your Spelling Notebook.

Skill: Children write a poem, using Spelling Words and Writer's Words from the Story.

REVIEW

Spelling Spree

SPELLING WORDS LESSON 5
took   good   cook
foot   book   look

✏ Finish each silly sentence. Write two Spelling Words that rhyme with the words in **dark print**.

_____

1. The man learned to _____ by

_____

reading a _____ near the **brook**.

_____

2. The fish _____ one

_____

_____ at the **hook** and **shook**.

✏ Write the Spelling Word that belongs in each group.

_____

3. toe, heel, _____

_____

4. nice, sweet, _____

Skill: Children review the spellings and meanings of words with the |o͝o| sound spelled *oo. See also* the Word Builder on page 67.

Theme 2 Old Favorites
REVIEW   **39**

REVIEW

Name _____ Lesson **8**

Spelling Spree

SPELLING WORDS LESSON 6		
soon	too	food
zoo	room	moon

✏ Write the missing Spelling Word to finish each news story title. Begin each word with a capital letter.

MOTHER GOOSE NEWS

1. Bo-peep Loses ____ Many Sheep!

2. Jack Sprat Will Not Eat His ____!

3. Mother Goose Visits Animals at the ____!

4. Jack Adds Another ____ to His House!

5. Cow Jumps over the ____!

6. Humpty Dumpty Will ____ Fall!

1. _____
2. _____
3. _____
4. _____
5. _____
6. _____

Skill: Children review the spellings and meanings of words with the |oo| sound spelled *oo*. *See also* the Word Builder on page 68.

Name _____ Lesson **8**

Spelling Spree

my	by	cry
try	fly	sky

✏️ Help Fox and Crow play a game. Write the Spelling
Word for each clue.

1. I am thinking of a word
that tells what jets do.

1. _____

2. I am thinking of a word
that tells what sad people do.

2. _____

3. I am thinking of a word
that begins like train.

3. _____

4. I am thinking of a word
that tells where clouds are.

4. _____

5. I am thinking of a word
that means near.

5. _____

6. I am thinking of a word
that begins like  .

6. _____

Skill: Children review the spellings and meanings of words with the
|ī| sound spelled *y. See also* the Word Builder on page 69.

Name _____ **Lesson 8**

Writer's Words Review

Writer's Words

went   house   water   first   thing
long   people   want   where

✏️ Write the Writer's Word for each clue.

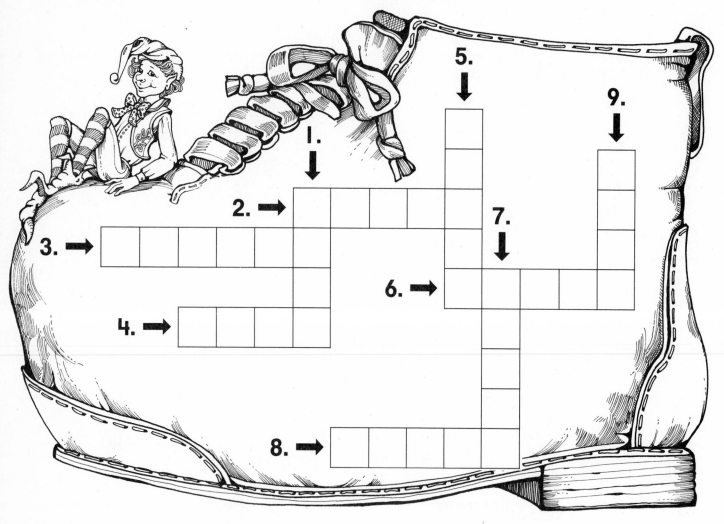

1. left
2. something you drink
3. men, women, and children
4. wish for
5. not last

6. rhymes with ring
7. a home
8. rhymes with there
9. not short

Skill: Children review the spellings and meanings of high-frequency words.

THEME 3

PROBLEMS, PROBLEMS!

Name _____

9 Double Consonants

LOOK at and **SAY** the words.

THINK about the words. Each word ends with two letters that are the same.

 Your Own Words

✏️ **WRITE** the missing letters to spell the ending sound in each Spelling Word. Then write each word.

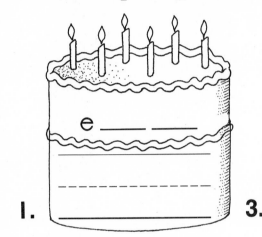

1.

2.

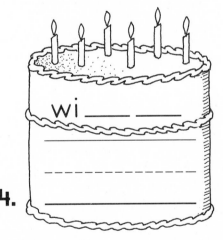

3.

4.

5.

6.

✏️ **WRITE** the two Spelling Words that end like 🏚️ .

7. _____

8. _____

CHECK the spelling of each word you wrote.

Skill: Children study the spellings of words that end with double consonants.

Theme 3 Problems, Problems!
THE BIRTHDAY CAKE   **45**

The Birthday Cake

Spelling and Meaning

SPELLING WORDS		
add	will	off
kiss	egg	tell

Write each word under the correct letter in your Spelling Notebook.

✎▷ Write the Spelling Word that can take the place of the words in **dark print**.

1. We **are going to** bake a cake.
2. I can **say to** you how to do it.
3. You can **put in** the flour.

_____   _____   _____

1. _____   2. _____   3. _____

Proofreading

✎▷ Circle three Spelling Words that are wrong. Write each word correctly.

I broke an ege!

Do not worry. I will clean it up. Give me a kis. Then hurry uff to school.

_____   _____   _____

4. _____   5. _____   6. _____

46   *Theme 3 Problems, Problems!*
THE BIRTHDAY CAKE

Skill: Children study the meanings of and proofread for spelling errors in words that end with double consonants.

Writer's Words from the Story

Writer's Words

which   think   here

Write each word under the correct letter in your Spelling Notebook.

✏️ Write the correct Writer's Words.

1.  _____

2. _____

3. 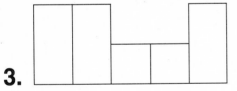 _____

✏️ Write the missing Writer's Words.

4. I am happy to see you all _____ !

5. I _____ you are good friends.

6. Tell me _____ box to open first.

Skill: Children study the spellings and meanings of high-frequency words.

Theme 3 Problems, Problems!
THE BIRTHDAY CAKE

Spelling and Writing

SPELLING WORDS		
add	will	off
kiss	egg	tell

Writer's Words	
which	think
here	

Think of two good friends. Draw a picture of each one.

Write the dates of their birthdays. Write what you might do for a birthday surprise. Use some list words.

Date

 **BIRTHDAY SURPRISE**

_____

- - - - - - - - - - - - - - - -

_____

- - - - - - - - - - - - - - - -

_____

Date

 **BIRTHDAY SURPRISE**

_____

- - - - - - - - - - - - - - - -

_____

- - - - - - - - - - - - - - - -

_____

 Write any hard words correctly in your Spelling Notebook.

Skill: Children write dates and descriptions, using Spelling Words and Writer's Words from the Story.

looked	rushing
looking	dressed
rushed	dressing

 Your Own Words

10 Adding ed and ing

LOOK at and **SAY** the words.

THINK about the words. What ending has been added to each action word?

✎ Make Spelling Words. Draw a stem from each flower to the basket below it.

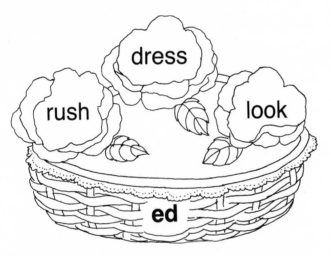

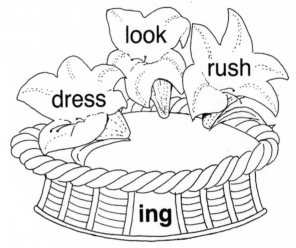

✎ **WRITE** the Spelling Words you made.

1. _____   3. _____   5. _____

2. _____   4. _____   6. _____

✎ **WRITE** the two Spelling Words that begin like 🚀 .

7. _____   8. _____

CHECK the spelling of each word you wrote.

Skill: Children study the spellings of verbs with the endings *-ed* and *-ing*.

Theme 3 Problems, Problems!
CARRY GO BRING COME

49

Carry Go Bring Come

Spelling and Meaning

SPELLING WORDS

looked rushed dressed
looking rushing dressing

Write each word under the correct letter in your Spelling Notebook.

✏️ Write the Spelling Word for each clue.

1. hurried

2. putting on clothes

3. watched

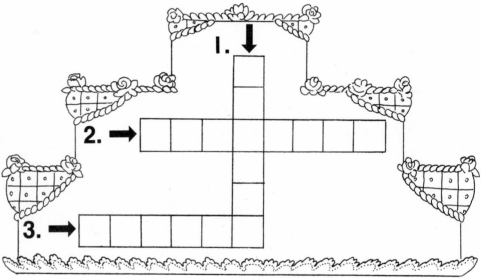

Proofreading

✏️ Circle three Spelling Words that are wrong. Write each word correctly.

Dear Uncle Bill,

Everyone was rushin around to get dresed. I looked at the cake. No one was loking at me!

Love,
Max

4. _____

_____

5. _____

_____

6. _____

Skill: Children study the meanings of and proofread for spelling errors in verbs with the endings -ed and -ing.

Writer's Words from the Story

Writer's Words
put   before   through

 Write each word under the correct letter in your Spelling Notebook.

✏️ Write the Writer's Word that begins like each picture name.

1. **3** _____

2. _____

3. _____

✏️ Write the missing Writer's Words.

How to Carry Everything at Once

- Get everything __4.__ you make your pile.

- Then __5.__ the big boxes on the bottom.

- Be sure you can fit __6.__ the doorway!

4. _____

5. _____

6. _____

Skill: Children study the spellings and meanings of high-frequency words.

Theme 3 Problems, Problems!
CARRY GO BRING COME

Spelling and Writing

SPELLING WORDS

looked rushed dressed
looking rushing dressing

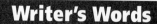

Writer's Words

put before
through

✏️▷ Newspapers have stories about weddings. Write a newspaper story about Leon's sister's wedding. Use some list words.

🖍️▷ Draw a picture to go with your story.

★ THE MORNING TIMES ★

[ruled writing lines with picture box on the right]

 Write any hard words correctly in your Spelling Notebook.

Skill: Children write a news story, using Spelling Words and Writer's Words from the Story.

Name _____

 Your Own Words

11 Adding es to Naming Words

LOOK at and **SAY** the words.

THINK about the words. What letters make each naming word mean more than one?

✏️ Add es to make each word mean more than one.
WRITE the Spelling Words you make.

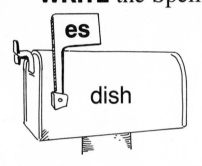

1. _____

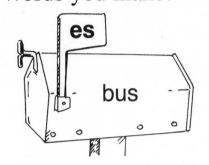

3. _____

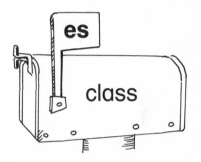

5. _____

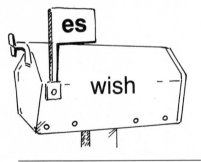

2. _____

4. _____

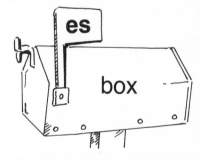

6. _____

✏️ **WRITE** the two Spelling Words that rhyme.

7. _____

8. _____

CHECK the spelling of each word you wrote.

Skill: Children study the spellings of nouns whose plural is formed by adding -es.

Theme 3 Problems, Problems!
ANNA'S SECRET FRIEND   **53**

Anna's Secret Friend

Spelling and Meaning

SPELLING WORDS		
boxes	wishes	buses
dishes	beaches	classes

Write each word under the correct letter in your Spelling Notebook.

✏️ Write the Spelling Word that belongs in each group.

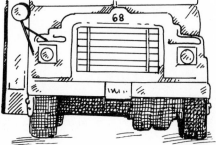

1. cars, trucks, _____

2. sand, waves, _____

3. cakes, candles, _____

_____ _____ _____

- -

1. _____ **2.** _____ **3.** _____

Proofreading

✏️ Circle three Spelling Words that are wrong. Write each word correctly.

 Friendship Day Plans

On Friendship Day, all clases will go on buses to visit new friends. They will bring dishez and food in boxis.

_____ _____ _____

- -

4. _____ **5.** _____ **6.** _____

Skill: Children study the meanings of and proofread for spelling errors in nouns whose plural is formed by adding *-es.*

Writer's Words from the Story

SPELLING WORDS

many   new   been

Write each word under the correct letter in your Spelling Notebook.

✏️ Write the Writer's Word for each clue.

1. It rhymes with few.

2. It ends like .

3. It rhymes with any.

1. _____   2. _____   3. _____

✏️ Write the missing Writer's Words.

🌸 Friend Finders Can Help You!

Have you __4.__ getting secret notes?
Do you want to find a __5.__ friend?
We help __6.__ people find friends!

4. _____   5. _____   6. _____

Skill: Children study the spellings and meanings of high-frequency words.

Theme 3 Problems, Problems!
ANNA'S SECRET FRIEND

Spelling and Writing

SPELLING WORDS		
boxes	wishes	buses
dishes	beaches	classes

Writer's Words

many   new

been

Pretend you just moved. Write a post card to tell a friend about your first day in your new home or new school. Use some list words.

TO:

 Write any hard words correctly in your Spelling Notebook.

Skill: Children write a post card, using Spelling Words and Writer's Words from the Story.

Name _____ Lesson **12**

Spelling Spree

SPELLING WORDS LESSON 9

| add | will | off |
| kiss | egg | tell |

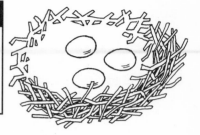

✏️ Write the missing Spelling Words.

_____

1. on and _____

2. hen and _____

3. take away or _____

✏️ Write the Spelling Word for each clue.

4. It rhymes with hill. It begins like .

5. It rhymes with miss. It begins like 👑.

6. It rhymes with bell. It begins like 🐯.

4. _____ **5.** _____ **6.** _____

Skill: Children review the spellings and meanings of words that end
with double consonants. *See also* the Word Builder on page 70.

Theme 3 Problems, Problems!
REVIEW **57**

Name _____ Lesson **12**

Spelling Spree

SPELLING WORDS LESSON 10

looked rushed dressed
looking rushing dressing

✏️ Add the ending to the words on each wheel. Write the Spelling Words you make.

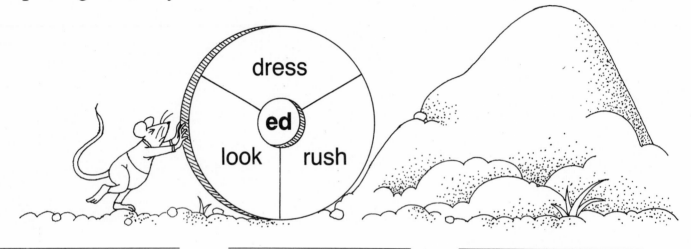

dress

ed

look   rush

1. _____   2. _____   3. _____

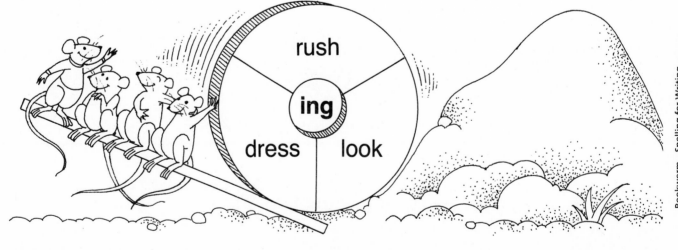

rush

ing

dress   look

4. _____   5. _____   6. _____

Skill: Children review the spellings of verbs with the endings *-ed* and *-ing. See also* the Word Builder on page 71.

Name _____ Lesson **12**

Spelling Spree

SPELLING WORDS LESSON 11

boxes   wishes   buses
dishes   beaches   classes

✏️ Write the Spelling Word to finish each answer.

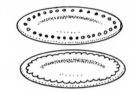 
1. + = 4 _____

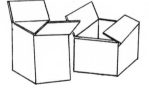
2. + = 2 _____

3. + = 3 _____

4. + = 2 _____

5. + = 3 _____

  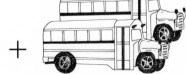 
6. + = 2 _____

Skill: Children review the spellings and meanings of nouns whose plural is formed by adding *-es*. See *also* the Word Builder on page 72.

Theme 3 Problems, Problems!
REVIEW

REVIEW

Name _____ Lesson **12**

Writer's Words Review

which	think	here	put	before
through	many	new	been	

✏️ Find out who helped Monkey. Use ABC order to draw a line from dot to dot. Then write the words in ABC order.

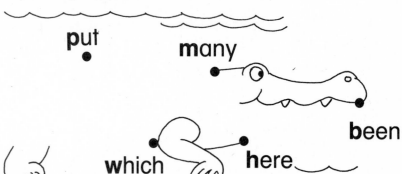

1. _____ 2. _____ 3. _____

4. _____ 5. _____ 6. _____

✏️ Circle three Writer's Words that are wrong. Write each word correctly. Begin each word with a capital letter.

Look Both Ways Befor Crossing Here.

Wrong Way! Find a Nu Path!

Go Thru the Other Door!

7. _____ 8. _____ 9. _____

Theme 3 Problems, Problems! REVIEW

Skill: Children review the spellings and meanings of high-frequency words.

Bookworm Spelling for Writing Copyright © Houghton Mifflin Company. All rights reserved.

STUDENT'S HANDBOOK

SPELLING NOTEBOOK

CONTENT AREA ACTIVITY SHEETS

TAKE-HOME LISTS

Name _____

Making ay Words

✎ Be a word builder. Use the letters in the picture to make five ay words. Then make your own ay word.

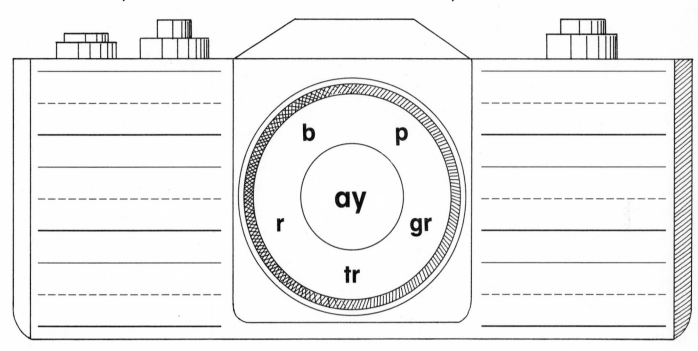

✎ Pretend you are on vacation. Write a post card to a friend. Use some ay words.

_____,

_____

_____

_____,

_____

Directions: Have children use these activities with **Review Lesson 4**, page 21. Note that children work together to complete the second activity.

Name _____

Making eat Words

✏️ Be a word builder. Use the letters in the picture to make six eat words.

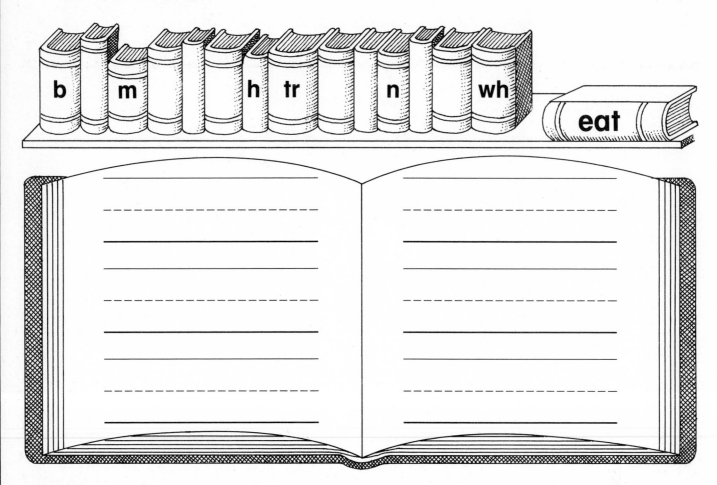

✏️ Write two eat words to answer each question.

What does good
music have?   a _____

What is a snack cracker?   a _____

Directions: Have children use these activities with **Review Lesson 4**, page 22.

Name _____

Making eam **Words**

✏️ Be a word builder. Use the letters in the picture to make six eam words.

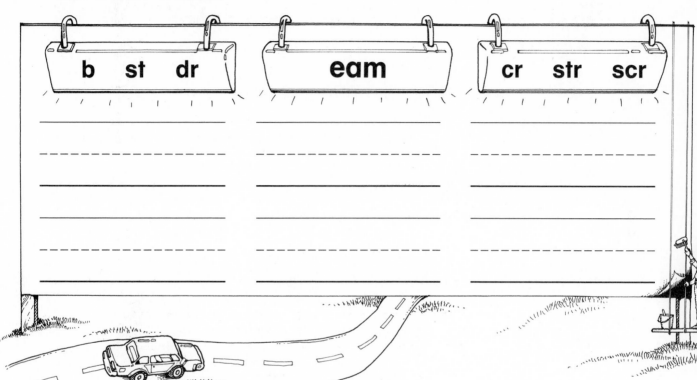

b st dr	eam	cr str scr

👥 Work with a friend. Make an ad for something you might buy. Use an eam word.

People scream for our ice cream!

Directions: Have children use these activities with **Review Lesson 4**, page 22. Note that children work together to complete the second activity.

Theme 1 People Who Write
WORD BUILDERS

Name _____

Adding s

✐ Write the answer to each riddle. Add s to a word in the box.

| monkey | elephant | bee | frog | dinosaur |

We have long tails and like
to swing. What are we?   _____

We lived long ago. We could be
as big as a house. What are we?   _____

We have wings and make honey.   _____
What are we?

✐ Add s to a word in the box. Write an animal riddle to go
with the word you made.

bear

duck

bird

tiger

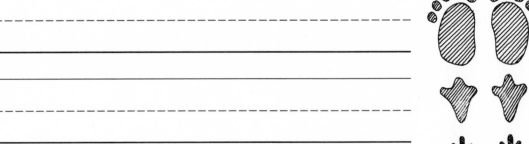
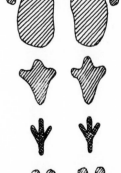

_____

_____

_____

_____

Answer: _____

✐ Write some more animal riddles on another sheet of paper.

Directions: Have children use these activities with **Review Lesson 4**,
page 23.

Name _____

Making ook and ood Words

✏️➤ Be a word builder. Use the letters in the picture to make six ook or ood words.

ook ood

br
sh
h

h
w
st

✏️➤ Get ready to write a fairy tale! Write three more ook and ood words.

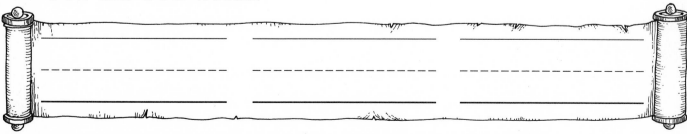

✏️➤ Now write your fairy tale on another sheet of paper. Use some ook and ood words.

Directions: Have children use these activities with **Review Lesson 8**, page 39.

Name _____

Making oon and oom Words

✏➤ Be a word builder. Color the apples that have letters you
   can use to build oon or oom words. Then write the words.

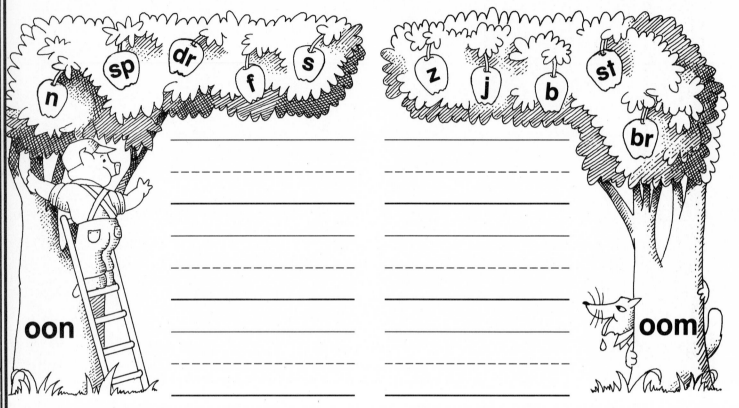

oon

oom

✏➤ Write what the pig and the wolf are thinking. Use some
   oon and oom words.

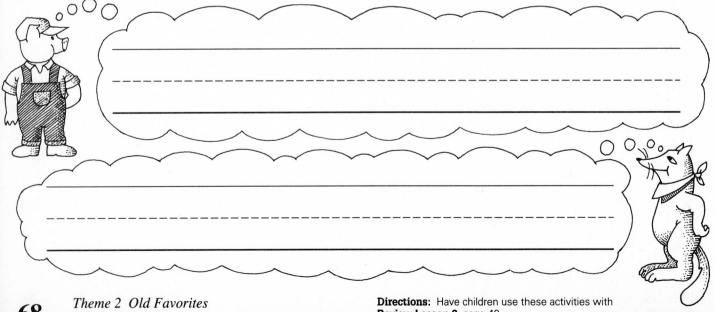

Directions: Have children use these activities with
Review Lesson 8, page 40.

Name _____

Making y Words

✏️➤ Help Jack build words that rhyme with try. Draw the correct path. Then write the words.

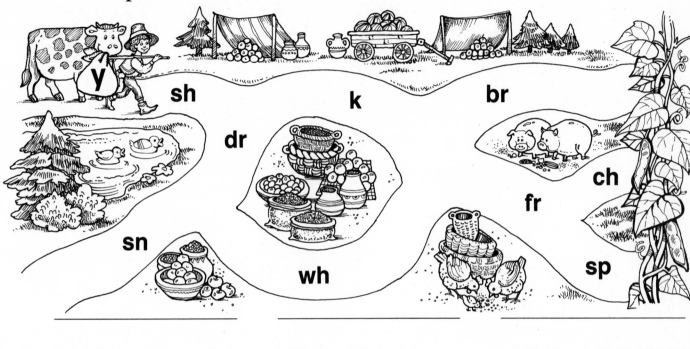

sh   k   br

dr

sn   wh   fr   ch

sp

_____ _____ _____

_____ _____ _____

_____ _____

_____ _____

✏️➤ Write three more words that rhyme with try.

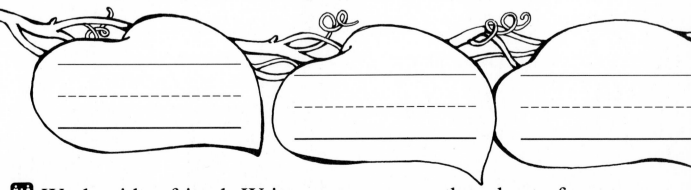

_____ _____ _____

👥 Work with a friend. Write a poem on another sheet of paper. Use some words that rhyme with try.

Directions: Have children use these activities with **Review Lesson 8**, page 41. Note that children work together to complete the third activity.

Theme 2 Old Favorites
WORD BUILDERS

Name _____

Making ill and ell Words

✏️ Be a word builder. Make an ill or an ell word for each picture in the story. Use the letters in the pictures.

Myrtle is missing! Maybe she took a

down the  . Maybe she into

the  . Maybe she went into her  !

_____ _____ _____

_____ _____

👥 Work with a friend. Write four more ill or ell words. Then write something else about Myrtle on another sheet of paper.

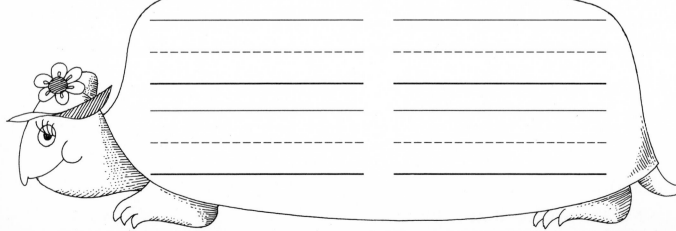

70 *Theme 3 Problems, Problems!*
WORD BUILDERS

Bookworm Spelling for Writing

Directions: Have children use these activities with **Review Lesson 12**, page 57. Note that children work together to complete the second activity.

Name _____

Adding ed and ing

✏️ Wendy had trouble building ed and ing words. She made this machine to help. Use it to add ed and ing to each word.

ed   fix
                          work   **ing**

_____   _____

_____   _____

_____   _____

_____

✏️ Pretend you built a machine. Tell how it helped you. Use a word from the box. Add ed or ing.

cook	add	clean	open	turn

_____

_____

_____

_____

🖍️ Draw a picture of your machine on another sheet of paper.

Directions: Have children use these activities with **Review Lesson 12**, page 58.

Theme 3 Problems, Problems!
WORD BUILDERS

Name _____

Adding es

✏️ Be a word builder. Add es to each word to finish the story.

| guess | dress | glass | fox | lunch |

_____   _____

Two _____ wearing _____

came to my house. It was noon. I put plates and

_____

_____ on the table. I didn't know what to make for

_____   _____

their _____ . Do you have any _____ ?

✏️ Tell what the foxes ate. Use a word from the box. Add es.

| bunch | squash | peach | mix |

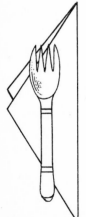
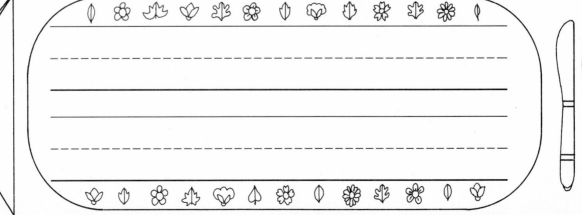

Directions: Have children use these activities with **Review Lesson 12**, page 59.

Bookworm Spelling for Writing

Name _____

Read your paper.

✓ Check your work.

☐ . ?

☐ CAPITAL LETTERS

☐ spelling

What else should you look for? Add it to your checklist.

☐ _____

Proofreading Hints

- Say each word. Be sure there are no missing letters.

- Read your paper to a friend.

- Circle the words you are not sure how to spell.
  Check the spelling of each circled word.

Proofreading Marks

Name _____

If you want to . . .	Use this mark.	Example
Add one or more words.	$\wedge$	I $\overset{have}{\underset{\wedge}{}}$ seen the play.
Take out one or more words. Change the spelling.	—	Kate ~~has~~ went home. The $\overset{balloon}{\sim}$ ~~baloon~~ popped.
Make a small letter a capital letter.	≡	My birthday is in june.
Make a capital letter a small letter.	/	My $\overset{d}{\cancel{D}}$og is brown.

74   PROOFREADING MARKS

Name _____

✏️ Trace and write the letters.

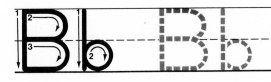

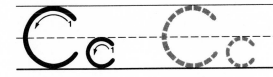

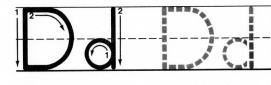

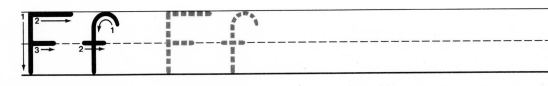

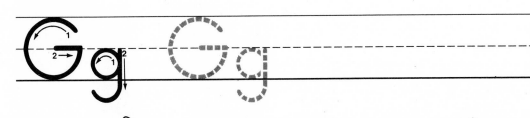

Aa   Bb   Cc   Dd   Ee   Ff   Gg

Name _____

✏️ Trace and write the letters.

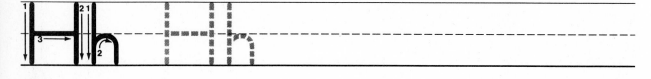

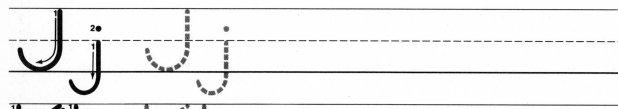

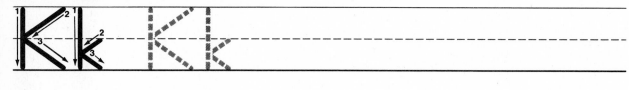

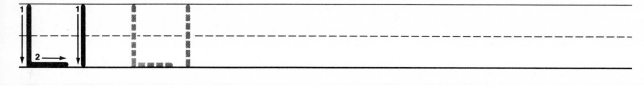

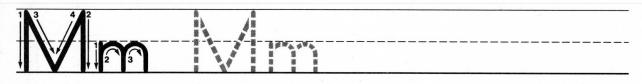

| Hh | Ii | Jj | Kk | Ll | Mm |

Name _____

 Trace and write the letters.

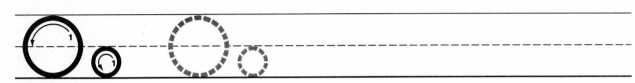

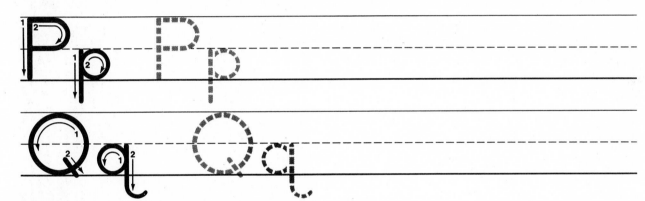

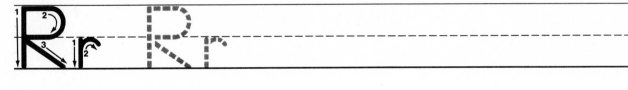

Nn   Oo   Pp   Qq   Rr   Ss

Name _____

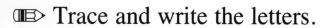 Trace and write the letters.

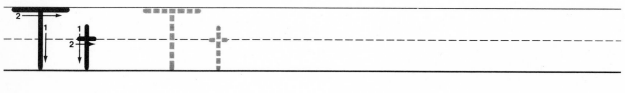

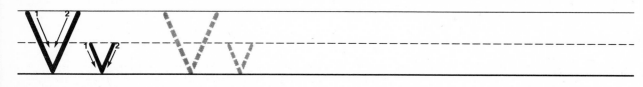

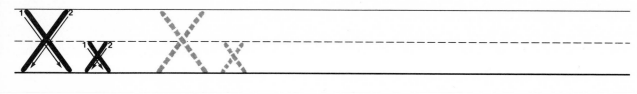

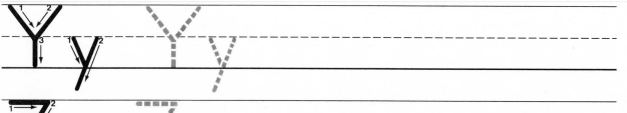

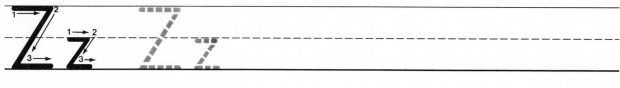

Tt   Uu   Vv   Ww   Xx   Yy   Zz

MY
SPELLING
NOTEBOOK

Name _____

Aa

Bb

Cc

b

Dd

C

d

E e

F f

G g

Hh

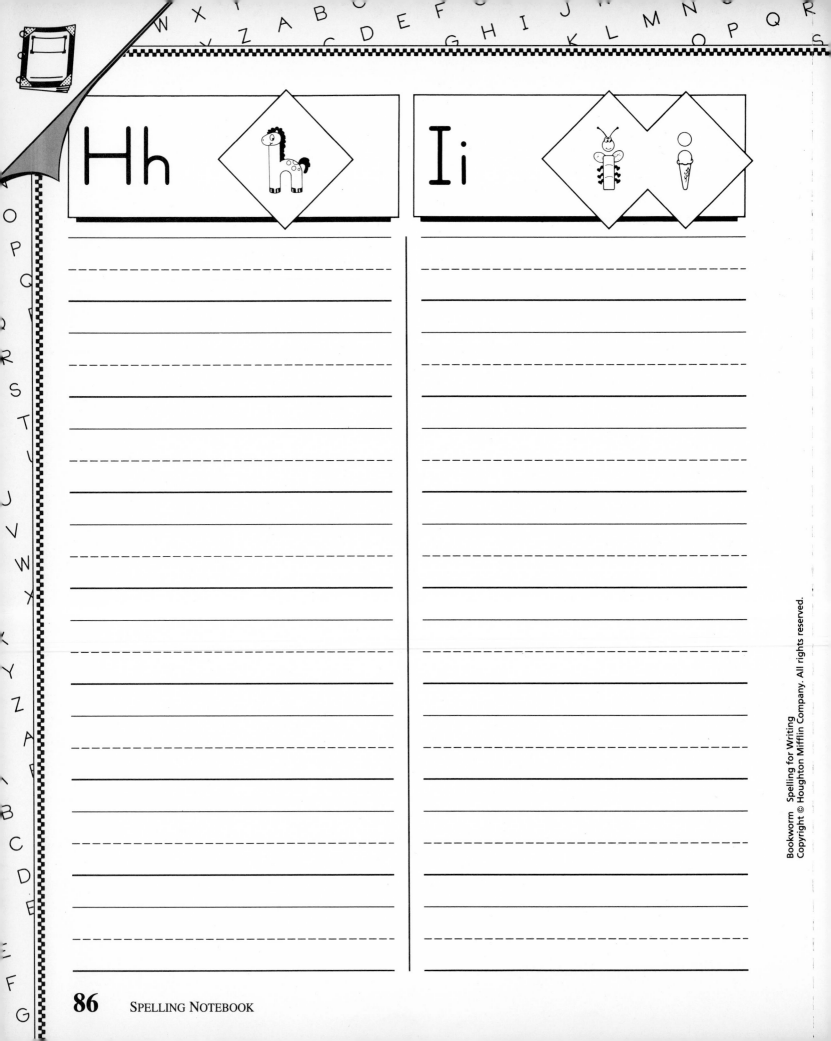

Ii

Bookworm Spelling for Writing
Copyright © Houghton Mifflin Company. All rights reserved.

J j

K k

Ll

Mm

SPELLING NOTEBOOK

N n

n

Oo

Pp

Qq

Rr

r

S s

S

S

T t

U u

V v

W w

Bookworm Spelling for Writing

Xx

W

Y y

Z z

Name _____

Names for Places

park
bank
store
school
library
pet shop

Directions: Have children draw, color, cut, and paste to complete
a map. *See* Teacher's Edition page T44 for instructions and
accompanying writing activity.

Name _____

Earth Day

earth	keep	save	water
dirty	litter	safe	air

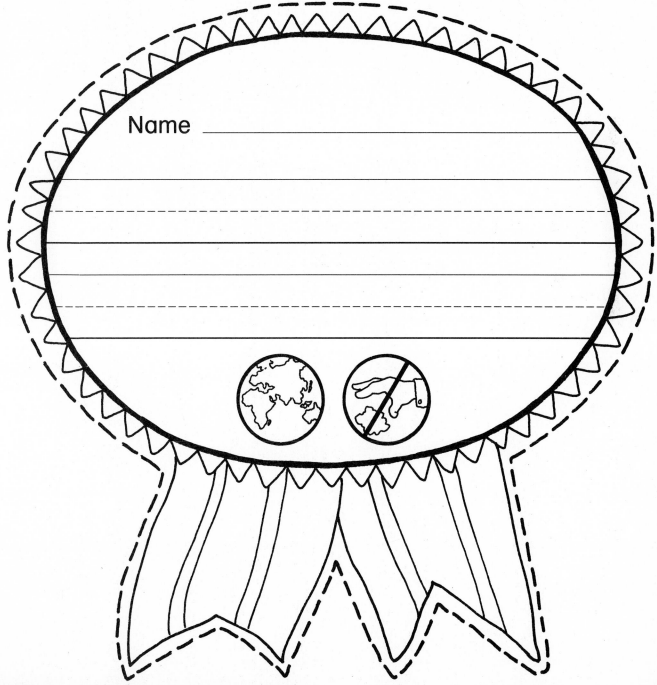

Name _____

Directions: Have children color, cut, and paste to make a "do not litter" badge and bag. *See* Teacher's Edition page T44 for instructions and accompanying writing activity.

Name _____

International Children's Book Day

| story | book | read | favorite | title | author |

Name _____

1. _____

2. _____

3. _____

4. _____

5. _____

6. _____

Directions: Have children cut, fold, and paste to make a bookmark for recording books they have read. *See* Teacher's Edition page T45 for instructions and accompanying writing activity.

Name _____

Family Words

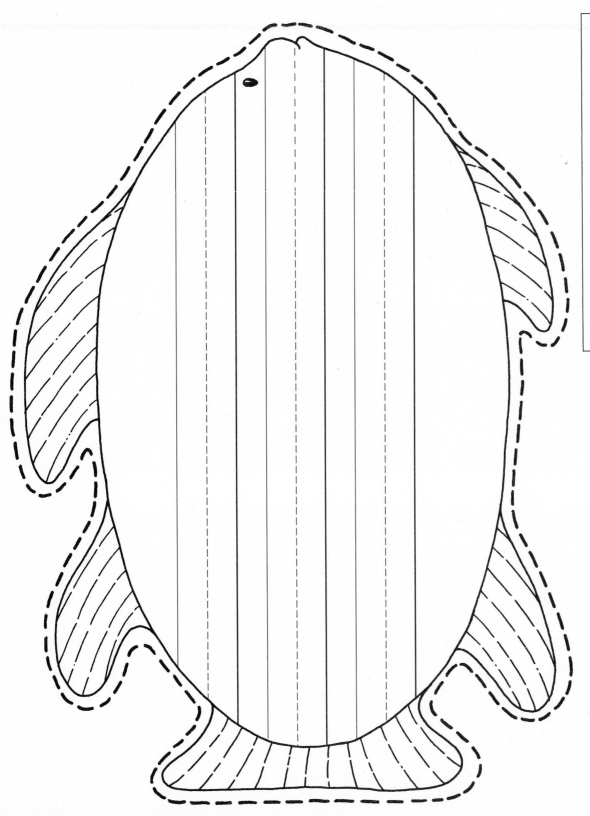

children
brother
sister
mother
father
family
helpful
kind

Directions: Have children color, paste, and cut to make a paper carp. *See* Teacher's Edition page T45 for instructions and accompanying writing activity.

Name _____

Rain Forest Words

frog
snake
monkey
lizard
parrot
butterfly
protect

Directions: Have children find and color the hidden rain forest animals. *See* Teacher's Edition page T46 for instructions and accompanying writing activity.

Name _____

Time Words

morning	night	hour	before
afternoon	o'clock	minutes	after

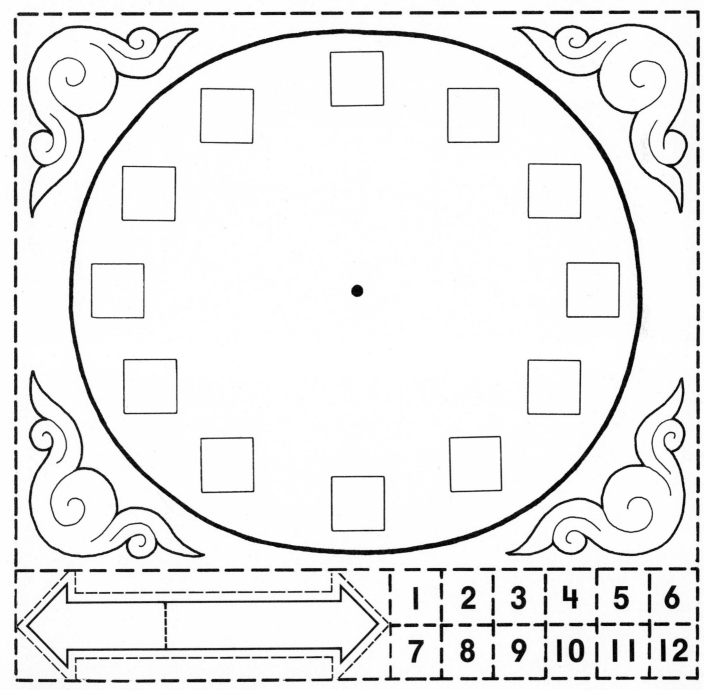

1	2	3	4	5	6
7	8	9	10	11	12

Directions: Have children cut, paste, assemble, and color a paper clock. *See* Teacher's Edition page T46 for instructions and accompanying writing activity.

Name _____

Take-Home Word List **1**

The Long a Sound Spelled ay

| way | day | play |

Spelling Words

1. way
2. day
3. play
4. say
5. stay
6. may

Challenge Words

1. away
2. today

Name _____

My Study List **1**

Spelling Words

_____
_____
_____
_____
_____
_____
_____
_____
_____
_____
_____
_____

Challenge Words

_____
_____
_____

Name _____

My Study List ▮1▮ (continued)

Writer's Words from the Story

_____

My Own Words

Name _____

Take-Home Word List ▮1▮ (continued)

Writer's Words from the Story
1. who
2. come
3. know

Name _____

Take-Home Word List 2

The Long e Sound Spelled ea

eat   r**ea**d   **ea**ch

Spelling Words

1. eat
2. read
3. each
4. team
5. seat
6. clean

Challenge Words

1. scream
2. please

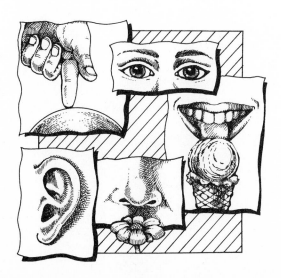

Name _____

My Study List 2

Spelling Words

_____

_____

_____

_____

_____

_____

_____

_____

_____

_____

_____

Challenge Words

_____

_____

_____

Name _____

My Study List 2 (continued)

Writer's Words from the Story

_____

- - - - - - - - - - - - - - - - - - -

_____

_____

_____

_____

_____

My Own
Words
· ·

_____

- - - - - - - - - - - - - - - - - - -

_____

_____

- - - - - - - - - - - - - - - - - - -

_____

_____

- - - - - - - - - - - - - - - - - - -

_____

114

Name _____

Take-Home Word List 2 (continued)

Writer's Words from the Story

1. or
2. how
3. because

◆ ◆ ◆ ◆ ◆ ◆ ◆ ◆ ◆ ◆ ◆ ◆ ◆ ◆ ◆ ◆

LOOK

SAY

THINK

WRITE

CHECK

Name _____

Take-Home Word List 3

Adding s to Naming Words

leg + **s** = leg**s**

cake + **s** = cake**s**

Spelling Words

1. legs
2. bats
3. seats
4. cakes
5. games
6. kites

Challenge Words

1. songs
2. stores

Name _____

My Study List 3

Spelling Words

_____
_____
_____
_____
_____
_____
_____
_____
_____
_____

Challenge Words

_____
_____
_____

Name _____

My Study List 3 (continued)

Writer's Words from the Story

_____
- -
_____
- -
_____
- -
_____

My Own Words

- -
_____
- -
_____
- -
_____
- -
_____

Name _____

Take-Home Word List 3 (continued)

Writer's Words from the Story

1. old
2. only
3. right

• • • • • • • • • • • • • • • • • • • •

LOOK

SAY

THINK

WRITE

CHECK

Name _____

Take-Home Word List 5

The Vowel Sound in book

t**oo**k   g**oo**d   c**oo**k

Spelling Words

1. took
2. good
3. cook
4. foot
5. book
6. look

Challenge Words

1. shook
2. stood

Name _____

My Study List 5

Spelling Words

_____

_____

_____

_____

_____

_____

_____

_____

_____

_____

Challenge Words

_____

_____

Name _____

My Study List **5** (continued)

Writer's Words from the Story

_____
- - - - - - - - - - - - - - - - - - -
_____
_____
_____
_____
_____

My Own Words

- - - - - - - - - - - - - - - - - - -
_____
_____
_____
_____
_____
_____
- - - - - - - - - - - - - - - - - - -

Name _____

Take-Home Word List **5** (continued)

Writer's Words from the Story

1. went
2. house
3. water

◆ ◆ ◆ ◆ ◆ ◆ ◆ ◆ ◆ ◆ ◆ ◆ ◆ ◆

LOOK

SAY

THINK

WRITE

CHECK

Name _____

Take-Home Word List 6

The Vowel Sound in moon

soon   t**oo**   f**oo**d

Spelling Words

1. soon
2. too
3. food
4. zoo
5. room
6. moon

Challenge Words

1. spoon
2. school

Name _____

My Study List 6

Spelling Words

_____
_____
_____
_____
_____
_____
_____
_____
_____
_____

Challenge Words

_____
_____
_____

Name _____

My Study List 6 (continued)

Writer's Words from the Story

_____

- - - - - - - - - - - - -

_____

- - - - - - - - - - - - -

_____

- - - - - - - - - - - - -

_____

My Own
Words
· ·

_____

- - - - - - - - - - - - -

_____

- - - - - - - - - - - - -

_____

- - - - - - - - - - - - -

_____

Name _____

Take-Home Word List 6 (continued)

Writer's Words from the Story
1. first
2. thing
3. long

◆ · ◆ · ◆ · ◆ · ◆ · ◆ · ◆ · ◆ · ◆ · ◆ · ◆

Name _____

Take-Home Word List 7

The Long i Sound Spelled y

| my | by | cry |

Spelling Words

1. my
2. by
3. cry
4. try
5. fly
6. sky

Challenge Words

1. why
2. July

Name _____

My Study List 7

Spelling Words

_____

_____

_____

_____

_____

_____

_____

Challenge Words

_____

_____

_____

Name _____

My Study List 7 (continued)

Writer's Words from the Story

_____

Name _____

Take-Home Word List 7 (continued)

Writer's Words from the Story
1. people
2. want
3. where

◆ ◆ ◆ ◆ ◆ ◆ ◆ ◆ ◆ ◆ ◆ ◆ ◆

My Own
Words

LOOK

SAY

THINK

WRITE

CHECK

Name _____

Take-Home Word List 9

Double Consonants

a**dd**	wi**ll**	o**ff**

Spelling Words

1. add
2. will
3. off
4. kiss
5. egg
6. tell

Challenge Words

1. smell
2. sniff

Name _____

My Study List 9

Spelling Words

_____
_____
_____
_____
_____
_____
_____
_____
_____
_____
_____

Challenge Words

_____
_____
_____

Name _____

My Study List 9 (continued)

Writer's Words from the Story

_____
- - - - - - - - - - - - - - - -
_____
_____
_____
_____
_____

My Own
..............Words..............
_____
- - - - - - - - - - - - - - - -
_____
_____
- - - - - - - - - - - - - - - -
_____
_____

Name _____

Take-Home Word List 9 (continued)

Writer's Words from the Story

1. which
2. think
3. here

◆ • ◆ • ◆ • ◆ • ◆ • ◆ • ◆ • ◆ • ◆ • ◆ • ◆ •

LOOK

SAY

THINK

WRITE

CHECK

Name _____

Take-Home Word List 10

Adding ed and ing
look + **ed** = look**ed**
look + **ing** = look**ing**

Spelling Words

1. looked
2. looking
3. rushed
4. rushing
5. dressed
6. dressing

Challenge Words

1. waited
2. waiting

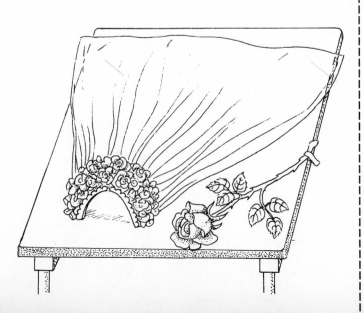

Name _____

My Study List 10

Spelling Words

_____

_____

_____

_____

_____

_____

_____

_____

_____

_____

_____

Challenge Words

_____

_____

_____

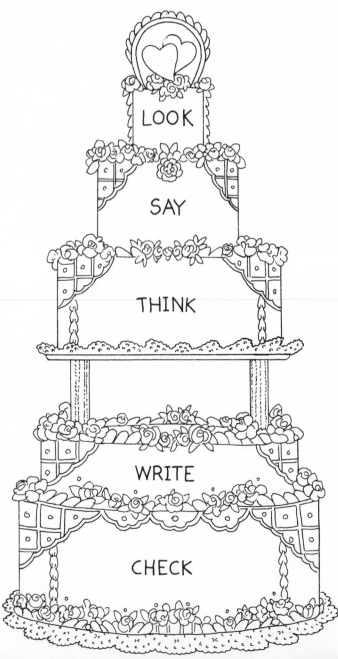
Name _____

My Study List 10 (continued)

Writer's Words from the Story

_____

- - - - - - - - - - - - - - - - - - - -

_____

- - - - - - - - - - - - - - - - - - - -

_____

- - - - - - - - - - - - - - - - - - - -

_____

My Own
Words

_____

- - - - - - - - - - - - - - - - - - - -

_____

- - - - - - - - - - - - - - - - - - - -

_____

- - - - - - - - - - - - - - - - - - - -

_____

Name _____

Take-Home Word List 10 (continued)

Writer's Words from the Story

1. put
2. before
3. through

LOOK

SAY

THINK

WRITE

CHECK

Bookworm Spelling for Writing

Name _____

Take-Home Word List 11

Adding es to Naming Words

box + **es** = box**es**

wish + **es** = wish**es**

Spelling Words

1. boxes
2. wishes
3. buses
4. dishes
5. beaches
6. classes

Challenge Words

1. bunches
2. guesses

Name _____

My Study List 11

Spelling Words

_____
_____
_____
_____
_____
_____
_____
_____
_____
_____
_____
_____

Challenge Words

_____
_____
_____

Name _____

My Study List **11** (continued)

Writer's Words from the Story

_____

_____

_____

My Own
Words

_____

_____

_____

Name _____

Take-Home Word List **11** (continued)

Writer's Words from the Story

1. many
2. new
3. been

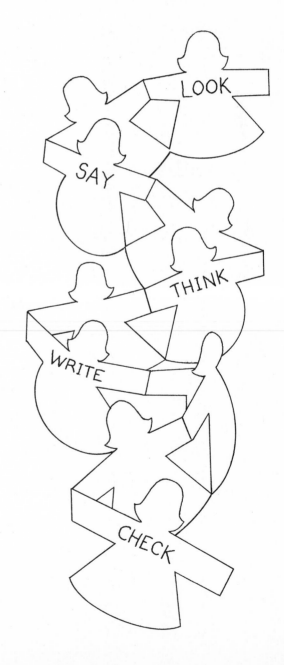

Bookworm Spelling for Writing